Flutter

Learning Flutter: A Beginner's Guide to Building Mobile Apps

Welcome to "Learning Flutter"

1

 # Flutter

Flutter

Flutter

4

 Chapter 1:

Introduction to Flutter

- **What is Flutter?**
- **Why choose Flutter for mobile app development?**
- **Setting up your development environment**
- **Hello World in Flutter: Your first app**

5

Chapter 1:
What is Flutter?

Flutter is an open-source UI software development kit created by Google. It allows developers to build natively compiled applications for mobile, web, and desktop from a single codebase. What sets Flutter apart is its ability to create beautiful, high-performance applications with a rich set of customizable widgets.

 Chapter 1:
Why Choose Flutter for Mobile App Development?

- **Fast Development**: Flutter's hot reload feature allows developers to see changes instantly, speeding up the development process.

- **Single Codebase**: With Flutter, you write one codebase that works across multiple platforms, saving time and effort.

 Chapter 1:

Why Choose Flutter for Mobile App Development?

- **Beautiful UIs**: Flutter offers a rich set of customizable widgets to create stunning user interfaces.

- **High Performance**: Flutter apps are compiled directly to native code, resulting in high performance and smooth animations.

Chapter 1:
Why Choose Flutter for Mobile App Development?

- **Growing Community:** Flutter has a vibrant community of developers, offering support, plugins, and resources.

Chapter 1:
Setting Up Your Development Environment

- Before you can start building Flutter apps, you need to set up your development environment. Follow these steps:

 Chapter 1:

Setting Up Your Development Environment

1. **Install Flutter SDK:** Download and install the Flutter SDK from the official website

https://flutter.dev/docs/get-started/install

Chapter 1:

Setting Up Your Development Environment

2.   Install Flutter IDE: Choose an Integrated Development Environment (IDE) for Flutter development. Popular choices include Android Studio, Visual Studio Code, and IntelliJ IDEA. Install the Flutter and Dart plugins/extensions for your chosen IDE.

 Chapter 1:

Setting Up Your Development Environment

3. Set Up Android Emulator or iOS Simulator: To run and test your Flutter apps, you'll need an Android emulator or iOS simulator. You can set up an Android emulator using Android Studio's AVD Manager or use a physical Android device. For iOS development, you'll need a Mac with Xcode installed to run the iOS simulator.

Chapter 1: Setting Up Your Development Environment

4. Verify Flutter Installation: Open a terminal or command prompt and run the command flutter doctor. This command checks your system for any missing dependencies and guides you on how to install them.

Congratulations! You've set up your Flutter development environment. Now, let's create your first Flutter app.

# Chapter 1:

Hello World in Flutter: Your First App

Open your chosen IDE and create a new Flutter project. Follow the prompts to choose a project name and location. Once your project is created, open the lib/main.dart file, which contains the main entry point for your app.

Replace the contents of main.dart with the following code:

# Chapter 1:
Hello World in Flutter:
Your First App

```dart
import 'package:flutter/material.dart';
void main() {
  runApp(MyApp()); }
class MyApp extends StatelessWidget {
  @override
  Widget build(BuildContext context) {
    return MaterialApp(
      home: Scaffold(
        appBar: AppBar(
          title: Text('Hello World') ),
          body: Center(
          child: Text(
            'Hello, Flutter!',
            style: TextStyle(fontSize:24.0),
          ), ), ), ); } }
```

Chapter 1:
Hello World in Flutter: Your First App

This code creates a simple Flutter app with a Material design scaffold containing an app bar and a centered text widget displaying "Hello, Flutter!".

 Chapter 1:
Hello World in Flutter: Your First App

To run your app, connect your device or start the emulator/simulator, and then run the app from your IDE. You should see your app running with the text "Hello, Flutter!" displayed on the screen.

Congratulations! You've successfully created and run your first Flutter app.

# Chapter 2:

Understanding Widgets

- **What are widgets in Flutter?**
- **Exploring different types of widgets**
- **Layout widgets: Row, Column, Stack, etc.**
- **Interactive widgets: Button, Textfield, Checkbox, etc.**

Chapter 2:

What are Widgets in Flutter?

In Flutter, everything is a widget. Whether it's a button, a layout, or even the entire app itself, each component in a Flutter app is represented by a widget. Widgets are objects responsible for constructing the user interface and determining how it responds to user interactions.

Widgets can be categorized into two main types:

 Chapter 2:

1. Stateless Widgets: Stateless widgets are immutable and do not maintain any state. They are useful for displaying static content that does not change over time.

2. Stateful Widgets: Stateful widgets are mutable and can maintain state throughout their lifetime. They are used for displaying dynamic content and responding to user interactions.

 Chapter 2:
Exploring Different Types of Widgets

Flutter provides a vast array of widgets that cater to various UI needs. Here are some common types of widgets you'll encounter:

Chapter 2:

1. Layout Widgets: Layout widgets are used to arrange other widgets on the screen. They determine how widgets are positioned and sized within the app's UI. Common layout widgets include:

Chapter 2:

- Row: Arranges its children widgets horizontally in a row.

- Column: Arranges its children widgets vertically in a column.

- Stack: Overlays its children widgets on top of each other.

- Container: A versatile widget for styling and positioning child widgets.

Chapter 2:

2. Interactive Widgets: Interactive widgets allow users to interact with the app by responding to user input. These widgets include:

 # Chapter 2:

- Button: Represents a clickable button that triggers an action when pressed.
- TextField: Allows users to input text through a keyboard.
- Checkbox: A widget that toggles between checked and unchecked states.
- Slider: Lets users select a value from a range by sliding a thumb along a track.

Chapter 2:

3. Material Widgets: Material widgets implement Material Design guidelines and provide a standard look and feel for Android apps. Examples include:

Chapter 2:

- AppBar: A toolbar displayed at the top of the screen.
- FloatingActionButton: A circular button typically used for primary actions.
- Card: A container with rounded corners, typically used to display content in a card-like format.

Chapter 2:

4. Cupertino Widgets: Cupertino widgets implement iOS-specific design patterns and provide a standard look and feel for iOS apps. Examples include:

Chapter 2:

- **CupertinoNavigationBar:** A navigation bar typically displayed at the top of the screen in iOS apps.
- **CupertinoButton:** A button styled according to iOS design conventions.
- **CupertinoTextField:** A text input field with iOS-style appearance.

 # Chapter 3:

Managing State

- **Introduction to state management in Flutter**
- **setState() method**
- **Stateful vs. Stateless widgets**
- **Using Provider package for state management**

 Chapter 3:
Introduction to State Management in Flutter

In Flutter, state refers to the data that influences the behavior and appearance of widgets in your app. State management involves managing and updating this data in response to user interactions, network requests, or other events.

State management is essential because it allows your app to maintain a consistent and up-to-date UI based on changing data and user input.

Chapter 3:
setState() Method

In Flutter, Stateful widgets are used when the UI needs to change dynamically based on internal state changes. The setState() method is a mechanism provided by Flutter to notify the framework that the internal state of a Stateful widget has changed, triggering a rebuild of the UI.

Here's a basic example of using setState() to update the UI:

Chapter 3:
setState() Method

```dart
import 'package:flutter/material.dart';

class CounterApp extends StatefulWidget {
  @override
  _CounterAppState createState() =>
_CounterAppState();
}


class _CounterAppState extends
State<CounterApp> {
  int _counter = 0;

  void _incrementCounter() {
    setState(() {
      _counter++;
    });
  }
```

Chapter 3:
setState() Method

```dart
@override
Widget build(BuildContext context) {
  return Scaffold(
    appBar: AppBar(
      title: Text('Counter App'),
    ),
    body: Center(
      child: Column(
        mainAxisAlignment:
MainAxisAlignment.center,
        children: <Widget>[
          Text(
            'Counter:',
          ),
          Text(
            '$_counter',
            style:
```

Chapter 3:
setState() Method

```dart
Theme.of(context).textTheme.headline4,
        ),
      ],
    ),
  ),
  floatingActionButton:
FloatingActionButton(
    onPressed: _incrementCounter,
    tooltip: 'Increment',
    child: Icon(Icons.add),
  ),
);
}
}
```

# Chapter 3:
setState() Method

In this example, pressing the floating action button triggers the "_incrementCounter()" method, which updates the "_counter" variable and calls "setState()" to notify Flutter that the UI needs to be rebuilt with the updated counter value.

 Chapter 3:
Stateful vs. Stateless Widgets

Stateful widgets maintain state that might change during the lifetime of the widget, while stateless widgets are immutable and do not change once built. When deciding between Stateful and Stateless widgets, consider whether the widget's appearance or behavior needs to change in response to events or data changes.

Chapter 3: Using Provider Package for State Management

While setState() works well for simple state management, more complex apps may require a more organized and scalable approach. The Provider package is a popular solution for managing app state in Flutter, offering a simple and efficient way to share and update state across the app.

Chapter 3:
Using Provider Package for State Management

Using Provider involves creating classes to hold the app's state and providing them to the widget tree using Provider widgets. This allows widgets to access and update the state without directly managing it.

 # Chapter 4:

Navigation and Routing

- Navigating between screens in Flutter
- Navigator widget
- Passing data between screens
- Named routes and routing

 Chapter 4:

Navigating Between Screens in Flutter

Flutter uses a stack-based navigation system, where each screen is pushed onto a navigation stack when navigated to and popped off the stack when navigated away from. The Navigator widget manages this navigation stack and provides methods for navigating between screens.

To navigate to a new screen, you can use the Navigator.push() method. To go back to the previous screen, you can use Navigator.pop().

Chapter 4:
Navigator Widget

The Navigator widget is the heart of navigation in Flutter. It maintains a stack of Route objects and provides methods for pushing, popping, and replacing routes.

Here's a basic example of navigating to a new screen using the Navigator widget:

 Chapter 4:
Navigator Widget

```dart
Navigator.push(
  context,
  MaterialPageRoute(builder: (context) =>
SecondScreen()),
);
```

Chapter 4: Passing Data Between Screens

Often, you'll need to pass data from one screen to another when navigating. Flutter provides a way to do this by passing arguments to the constructor of the new screen.

 # Chapter 4:
Passing Data Between Screens

```dart
Navigator.push(
  context,
  MaterialPageRoute(
    builder: (context) => SecondScreen(data:
'Hello from FirstScreen'),
  ),
);
```

# Chapter 4:
Passing Data Between Screens

In the SecondScreen, you can access this data:

 # Chapter 4: Passing Data Between Screens

```dart
class SecondScreen extends StatelessWidget {
  final String data;

  SecondScreen({required this.data});

  @override
  Widget build(BuildContext context) {
    return Scaffold(
      appBar: AppBar(
        title: Text('Second Screen'),
      ),
      body: Center(
        child: Text(data),
      ),
    );
}}
```

 Chapter 4:
Named Routes and Routing

Named routes provide a way to define routes using a named identifier, making navigation more declarative and easier to manage, especially in larger apps.

```dart
MaterialApp(
  routes: {
    '/': (context) => HomeScreen(),
    '/second': (context) => SecondScreen(),
  },
);
```

Chapter 4:
Named Routes and Routing

To navigate using named routes:

```dart
Navigator.pushNamed(context, '/second');
```

 # Chapter 5:

Working with APIs

- Making HTTP requests in Flutter
- Fetching data from REST APIs
- Parsing JSON data
- Displaying fetched data in your app

Chapter 5:
Making HTTP Requests in Flutter

Flutter provides the http package for making HTTP requests. This package allows you to communicate with RESTful APIs to fetch data from external servers.

Here's a basic example of making an HTTP GET request:

 Chapter 5:
Making HTTP Requests in Flutter

```dart
import 'package:http/http.dart' as http;

Future<void> fetchData() async {
  final response = await
http.get(Uri.parse('https://api.example.com/
data'));
  if (response.statusCode == 200) {
    // Data fetched successfully
    print(response.body);
  } else {
    // Error fetching data
    print('Failed to fetch data:
${response.statusCode}');
  }
}
```

Chapter 5:
Fetching Data from REST APIs

Once you've made an HTTP request and received a response, you can extract and process the data returned by the API. Most REST APIs return data in JSON format, which you can parse and convert into Dart objects.

Chapter 5:
Parsing JSON Data

Flutter provides built-in support for working with JSON data using the dart:convert package. You can use the jsonDecode() function to parse JSON strings into Dart objects and vice versa. Here's an example of parsing JSON data fetched from an API:

Chapter 5:
Parsing JSON Data

```dart
import 'dart:convert';

void parseJson(String jsonString) {
  final Map<String, dynamic> data =
jsonDecode(jsonString);
  // Access data using key-value pairs
  print(data['key']);
}
```

Chapter 5:
Displaying Fetched Data in Your App

Once you've fetched and parsed the data, you can display it in your app's user interface using Flutter widgets. Depending on the structure of your data, you may use widgets like ListView, GridView, or Text to present the data to the user.

Here's a simple example of displaying a list of items fetched from an API using a ListView:

Chapter 5: Displaying Fetched Data in Your App

```dart
ListView.builder(
  itemCount: data.length,
  itemBuilder: (context, index) {
    return ListTile(
      title: Text(data[index]['title']),
      subtitle: Text(data[index]
['subtitle']),
    );
  },
);
```

Chapter 5:
Displaying Fetched Data in Your App

dart

```dart
ListView.builder(
  itemCount: data.length,
  itemBuilder: (context, index) {
    return ListTile(
      title: Text(data[index]['title']),
      subtitle: Text(data[index]
['subtitle']),
    );
  },
);
```

 # Chapter 6:

Handling User Input

- Getting user input using text fields
- Validating user input Input
- masks and form submission
- Working with gestures: onTap, onLongPress, etc.

 # Chapter 6:

Handling User Input

Handling user input is fundamental to creating interactive apps. In this chapter, you'll learn how to get input from text fields, validate user input, use input masks and forms, and work with gestures.

Chapter 6:
Getting User Input Using Text Fields

Text fields are commonly used to collect user input in forms. Flutter provides the TextField widget to capture user input. Here's an example of a simple text field:

Chapter 6:
Getting User Input Using Text Fields

```dart
TextField(
  decoration: InputDecoration(
    labelText: 'Enter your name',
  ),
  onChanged: (value) {
    print('Input: $value');
  },
)
```

- **InputDecoration:** Adds a label or hint to the text field.

- **onChanged:** A callback that captures changes to the text input.

Chapter 6:
Validating User Input

Validating user input ensures that the provided data is accurate and follows required guidelines. Flutter provides the TextFormField widget, which works well with forms and validation.

Here's an example of validating a text field:

Chapter 6:
Validating User Input

```dart
final _formKey = GlobalKey<FormState>();

Form(
  key: _formKey,
  child: Column(
    children: [
      TextFormField(
        decoration:
InputDecoration(labelText: 'Email'),
        validator: (value) {
          if (value == null ||
value.isEmpty) {
            return 'Please enter your
email';
          } else if (!value.contains('@')) {
            return 'Invalid email format';
          }
          return null;
```

Chapter 6:
Validating User Input

```dart
        },
      ),
      ElevatedButton(
        onPressed: () {
          if
(_formKey.currentState!.validate()) {
            print('Form submitted
successfully');
          }
        },
        child: Text('Submit'),
      ),
    ],
  ),
)
```

Chapter 6:
Input Masks and Form Submission

Input masks ensure that users enter data in the correct format. For example, a phone number should follow a specific pattern. You can use external packages like flutter_masked_text or intl_phone_number_input to achieve this.

For form submission, ensure that the form passes validation before processing the input data.

Chapter 6:
Working with Gestures: onTap, onLongPress, etc.

Gestures such as taps and long presses can make your app more interactive. Flutter's gesture detection system makes it easy to detect and handle these gestures.

1. onTap: Triggered when a widget is tapped.
2. onLongPress: Triggered when a widget is long-pressed.

Here's an example of working with gestures:

# Chapter 6:

Working with Gestures:
onTap, onLongPress, etc.

```dart
GestureDetector(
  onTap: () {
    print('Widget tapped');
  },
  onLongPress: () {
    print('Widget long-pressed');
  },
  child: Container(
    padding: EdgeInsets.all(20),
    color: Colors.blueAccent,
    child: Text(
      'Tap or Long Press',
      style: TextStyle(color: Colors.white),
    ),
  ),
)
```

 # Chapter 6:

Working with Gestures: onTap, onLongPress, etc.

- **GestureDetector**: A widget that detects various gestures.
- **onTap** and **onLongPress**: Callbacks executed when gestures are detected.

 # Chapter 7:

Styling and Theming

- **Styling your Flutter app with themes**
- **Customizing colors, fonts, and shapes**
- **Theming your app for light and dark mode**
- **Using external packages for advanced styling**

Chapter 7: Styling and Theming

Creating a consistent look and feel for your Flutter app is crucial for user experience. In this chapter, you'll learn how to style your app using themes, customize colors and fonts, implement light and dark modes, and leverage external packages for more advanced styling.

 Chapter 7:

Styling Your Flutter App with Themes

A theme defines your app's overall visual style, such as colors, fonts, and shapes. Flutter's ThemeData class allows you to specify default styles that apply throughout your app.

Here's an example of applying a theme to your app:

Chapter 7: Styling Your Flutter App with Themes

```dart
MaterialApp(
  title: 'Themed App',
  theme: ThemeData(
    primarySwatch: Colors.blue,
    textTheme: TextTheme(
      headline1: TextStyle(fontSize: 36.0,
fontWeight: FontWeight.bold),
      bodyText2: TextStyle(fontSize: 14.0,
color: Colors.grey[600]),
    ),
    buttonTheme: ButtonThemeData(
      buttonColor: Colors.blue,
      textTheme: ButtonTextTheme.primary,
    ),
  ),
  home: MyHomePage(),)
```

 # Chapter 7:
Styling Your Flutter App with Themes

- **primarySwatch**:
Sets the primary color used throughout the app.

- **textTheme**:
Defines global text styles for different text elements.

- **buttonTheme**:
Provides consistent button styles.

Chapter 7:
Customizing Colors, Fonts, and Shapes

You can further customize the appearance of individual widgets using the widget's specific properties or by using themes.

Chapter 7:
Customizing Colors, Fonts, and Shapes

1. **Colors:** Use the color property of a widget to customize its color:

```dart
Container(
  color: Colors.green,
  child: Text('Custom Colored Container'),
)
```

# Chapter 7:

Customizing Colors, Fonts, and Shapes

2. Fonts: To apply custom fonts, include the font files in the pubspec.yaml file under fonts, and set the font family in the widget:

```dart
Text(
  'Custom Font Text',
  style: TextStyle(
    fontFamily: 'Roboto',
    fontSize: 24.0,
  ),
)
```

 # Chapter 7:
Customizing Colors, Fonts, and Shapes

3. Shapes: Customize widget shapes with properties like borderRadius, shape, and more:

```dart
Container(
  decoration: BoxDecoration(
    borderRadius:
BorderRadius.circular(15.0),
    color: Colors.orange,
  ),
  child: Text('Rounded Container'),
)
```

Chapter 7: Theming Your App for Light and Dark Mode

Support for light and dark mode enhances the user experience. Flutter makes it easy to switch themes based on the device's current brightness.

Chapter 7:
Theming Your App for Light and Dark Mode

```dart
MaterialApp(
  title: 'Adaptive Themed App',
  theme: ThemeData.light(),
  darkTheme: ThemeData.dark(),
  themeMode: ThemeMode.system, //
Automatically switch based on system setting
  home: MyHomePage(),
)
```

- **ThemeMode.system**: Automatically switches between light and dark themes based on the system setting

81

 Chapter 7:

Using External Packages for Advanced Styling

Flutter's ecosystem provides packages for advanced styling. Here are some useful ones:

1. Google Fonts:

Access Google's font library effortlessly.

```dart
import
'package:google_fonts/google_fonts.dart';
Text(
  'Google Fonts Text',
  style: GoogleFonts.lato(fontSize: 24.0),
)
```

# Chapter 7:

Using External Packages for Advanced Styling

2. **Flutter Spinkit**: A collection of loading indicators.

```dart
import 'package:lottie/lottie.dart';

Lottie.asset('assets/animation.json')
```

Chapter 7: Using External Packages for Advanced Styling

3. Lottie: Add high-quality animations to your app.

```dart
import
'package:flutter_spinkit/flutter_spinkit.dart';

SpinKitFadingCube(color: Colors.blue)
```

 # Chapter 8:

Animations and Effects

- Introduction to animations in Flutter
- Animating widgets: Tween, AnimatedBuilder, etc.
- Creating custom animations
- Adding visual effects to your app

Chapter 8: Animations and Effects

In this chapter, we'll explore animations and visual effects in Flutter, enhancing the user experience and making your app more engaging. We'll cover the basics of animations, animating widgets using Tween and AnimatedBuilder, creating custom animations, and adding visual effects to your app.

Chapter 8:
Introduction to Animations in Flutter

Animations bring life to your app by adding movement and interactivity. Flutter provides a powerful animation framework that allows you to create smooth and visually appealing animations with ease.

 Chapter 8:

Animating Widgets: Tween, AnimatedBuilder, etc.

1- **Tween Animation**: Tween animations interpolate between two values over a specified duration. Flutter provides the Tween class to define the range of values for the animation and the TweenAnimationBuilder widget to animate a widget based on the tween's value.

 Chapter 8:

Animating Widgets: Tween, AnimatedBuilder, etc.

```dart
TweenAnimationBuilder<double>(
  tween: Tween(begin: 0.0, end: 1.0),
  duration: Duration(seconds: 1),
  builder: (context, value, child) {
    return Opacity(
      opacity: value,
      child: child,
    );
  },
  child: Text('Fade In Animation'),
)
```

 # Chapter 8:

Animating Widgets: Tween, AnimatedBuilder, etc.

2- AnimatedBuilder: The AnimatedBuilder widget allows you to create complex animations by explicitly controlling the animation and building the widget tree in response to the animation's value changes.

 # Chapter 8:

Animating Widgets: Tween, AnimatedBuilder, etc.

```dart
AnimatedBuilder(
  animation: _controller,
  builder: (context, child) {
    return Transform.rotate(
      angle: _controller.value * 2 * pi,
      child: FlutterLogo(size: 100),
    );
  },
)
```

 Chapter 8:
Creating Custom Animations

Flutter enables you to create custom animations tailored to your app's specific requirements. You can use the Animation class and its subclasses to define custom animations and control their behavior programmatically.

Chapter 8:
Adding Visual Effects to Your App

In addition to animations, you can enhance your app's visual appeal by adding various effects such as shadows, gradients, blurs, and more. Flutter provides widgets and properties to apply these effects to your app's UI elements.

# Chapter 8:

Adding Visual Effects to Your App

```dart
Container(
  decoration: BoxDecoration(
    color: Colors.blue,
    boxShadow: [
      BoxShadow(
        color:
Colors.black.withOpacity(0.5),
        blurRadius: 5.0,
        spreadRadius: 2.0,
        offset: Offset(2.0, 2.0),
      ),
    ],
```

Chapter 8:
Adding Visual Effects to Your App

```dart
  gradient: LinearGradient(
    colors: [Colors.red, Colors.blue],
    begin: Alignment.topCenter,
    end: Alignment.bottomCenter,
  ),
),
child: Text('Visual Effects'),
)
```

 # Chapter 9:

Handling Images and Assets

- Loading and displaying images in Flutter
- Asset management in Flutter
- Caching and optimizing images
- Using SVG and other vector formats

Chapter 9:

Handling Images and Assets

In this chapter, we'll dive into handling images and assets in your Flutter app. We'll cover loading and displaying images, asset management, caching and optimizing images for better performance, and working with SVG and other vector formats.

 Chapter 9:

Loading and Displaying Images in Flutter

Flutter provides the Image widget to load and display images in your app. You can load images from various sources, including assets, network URLs, and local files.

```dart
Image.asset
('assets/images/flutter_logo.png')
```

Chapter 9:

Asset Management in Flutter

Assets are resources bundled with your app, such as images, fonts, and JSON files. To include assets in your Flutter app, declare them in the pubspec.yaml file:

```dart
flutter:
  assets:
    - assets/images/flutter_logo.png
```

 # Chapter 9:

Asset Management in Flutter

You can then access these assets using the AssetImage class:

```dart
Image(image:
AssetImage('assets/images/flutter_logo.png')
)
```

 Chapter 9:
Caching and Optimizing Images

To improve app performance and reduce network usage, Flutter provides caching mechanisms for images. The cached_network_image package allows you to load images from network URLs with caching support:

 # Chapter 9:

Caching and Optimizing Images

```dart
CachedNetworkImage(
  imageUrl: 'https://example.com/image.jpg',
)
```

For local images, you can use the flutter_cache_manager package to cache images fetched from assets or network URLs.

 Chapter 9:

Using SVG and Other Vector Formats

Vector graphics formats like SVG offer scalability and flexibility compared to raster images. Flutter supports rendering SVG images using the flutter_svg package:

# Chapter 9:

Using SVG and Other Vector Formats

```dart
SvgPicture.asset(
  'assets/images/vector_image.svg',
  semanticsLabel: 'Vector Image',
)
```

You can also use other vector formats like PDF and EPS with appropriate Flutter plugins or packages.

# Chapter 10:

Flutter Testing and Debugging

- Writing unit tests for your Flutter app
- Debugging techniques in Flutter
- Using Flutter DevTools for debugging
- Testing your app on different devices and screen sizes

Chapter 10: Flutter Testing and Debugging

Testing and debugging are critical aspects of app development to ensure reliability and identify and fix issues. In this chapter, we'll explore writing unit tests, debugging techniques, utilizing Flutter DevTools, and testing your app on different devices and screen sizes.

Chapter 10:

Writing Unit Tests for Your Flutter App

Unit tests verify the functionality of individual units of code, such as functions and classes, in isolation. Flutter provides a testing framework for writing and running unit tests.

Chapter 10:

Writing Unit Tests for Your Flutter App

Example unit test:

```dart
void main() {
  test('String should contain hello', () {
    String greeting = getGreeting();
    expect(greeting.contains('hello'),
true);
  });
}
```

 Chapter 10:

Debugging Techniques in Flutter

Flutter offers various debugging techniques to identify and resolve issues during development:

1- **Print Statements**: Adding print statements to your code to log variable values and execution flow.

Chapter 10:
Debugging Techniques in Flutter

2- **Debugging Tools**: Using Flutter's built-in debugging tools, such as the Flutter Inspector and Debug Paint, to visualize widget hierarchy and layout.

3- **Breakpoints**: Setting breakpoints in your code to pause execution and inspect variable values and stack traces.

Chapter 10: Debugging Techniques in Flutter

4- Logging: Utilizing logging libraries like logger or logging to log messages with different severity levels.

Chapter 10:
Using Flutter DevTools for Debugging

Flutter DevTools is a suite of performance and debugging tools that provides insights into your Flutter app's behavior and performance. It includes tools for profiling, debugging, inspecting widget hierarchy, and more.

Chapter 10:
Using Flutter DevTools for Debugging

To launch Flutter DevTools:

```dart
flutter pub global activate devtools
flutter pub global run devtools
```

Chapter 10:

Testing Your App on Different Devices and Screen Sizes

Flutter's device preview feature allows you to visualize how your app will look on different devices and screen sizes directly within your IDE. You can select various device configurations to preview your app's layout and responsiveness.

```dart
flutter run --device-id <device-id>
```

Chapter 11: Deploying Your App

- Building and packaging your Flutter app
- Publishing your app to Google Play Store and Apple App Store
- App signing and release management
- Continuous integration and delivery (CI/CD) for Flutter apps

Chapter 11: Deploying Your App

Deploying your Flutter app to the Google Play Store and Apple App Store marks the culmination of your development efforts. In this chapter, we'll cover building and packaging your Flutter app, publishing it to both stores, managing app signing and release processes, and implementing Continuous Integration and Delivery (CI/CD) for seamless app deployment.

 Chapter 11:

Building and Packaging Your Flutter App

Before deploying your app, you need to build and package it for distribution. Flutter provides commands to build your app for specific platforms:

 Chapter 11:

Building and Packaging Your Flutter App

For Android:

```dart
flutter build apk
```

For IOS:

```dart
flutter build ios
```

These commands generate APK (Android) or IPA (iOS) files ready for distribution.

Chapter 11:

Publishing Your App to Google Play Store and Apple App Store

1- Google Play Store:

Chapter 11:
Publishing Your App to Google Play Store and Apple App Store

- Generate a signing key using Android Studio or the keytool command.

- Configure your Flutter app's android/app/build.gradle file with the signing configuration.

- Build the release APK using flutter build apk.

- Upload the APK to the Google Play Console and follow the publishing process.

 Chapter 11:

Publishing Your App to Google Play Store and Apple App Store

2- Apple App Store:

Chapter 11: Publishing Your App to Google Play Store and Apple App Store

- Create an App ID and provisioning profile in the Apple Developer Center.

- Configure your Flutter app's iOS settings in Xcode.

- Build and archive your app using Xcode.

- Submit the archive to App Store Connect and follow the review and release process.

Chapter 11:

App Signing and Release Management

App signing ensures the authenticity and integrity of your app. For Android, you sign your app using a keystore file. For iOS, Xcode handles signing during the build process.

Chapter 11:

App Signing and Release Management

Release management involves managing app versions, release notes, and rollout strategies. Google Play Console and App Store Connect provide tools for managing releases and distribution.

 Chapter 11:

Continuous Integration and Delivery (CI/CD) for Flutter Apps

CI/CD automates the build, testing, and deployment processes, ensuring that changes are integrated smoothly and reliably into the app's production environment.

Chapter 11:

Continuous Integration and Delivery (CI/CD) for Flutter Apps

Popular CI/CD services like GitHub Actions, Bitrise, and Codemagic support Flutter apps. You can set up workflows to automatically build, test, and deploy your app whenever changes are pushed to your repository.

Chapter 12: Building a Complete App

- Building a real-world app from scratch
- Applying all the concepts learned throughout the book
- Designing the app UI and functionality
- Testing and debugging the app

Chapter 12: Building a Complete App

In this final chapter, we'll embark on the journey of building a complete real-world Flutter app from scratch. We'll apply all the concepts learned throughout the book, focusing on designing the app UI and functionality, testing, and debugging.

Chapter 12:

Planning Your App

Before diving into coding, it's essential to plan your app's features, user interface, and overall architecture. Consider creating wireframes or sketches to visualize your app's layout and flow. Define the core functionalities and prioritize them based on user needs.

Chapter 12:

Designing the App UI and Functionality

Start by designing the user interface (UI) of your app using Flutter's rich set of widgets and material design principles. Implement the app's layout, navigation structure, and interactive elements such as buttons, text fields, and lists.

Chapter 12:

Designing the App UI and Functionality

Next, implement the app's functionality, including data fetching, state management, and user interactions. Use appropriate design patterns such as MVC (Model-View-Controller) or MVVM (Model-View-ViewModel) to maintain a clean and organized codebase.

Chapter 12:

Testing and Debugging the App

Throughout the development process, write unit tests to ensure that individual components of your app behave as expected. Test edge cases and handle error scenarios gracefully.

Chapter 12:

Testing and Debugging the App

Utilize Flutter's debugging tools, such as print statements, breakpoints, and Flutter DevTools, to debug and diagnose issues during development. Pay attention to performance optimizations and address any performance bottlenecks.

Chapter 12:

Continuous Iteration and Improvement

Building a complete app is just the beginning. Continuously gather user feedback, monitor app analytics, and iterate based on user needs and preferences. Regularly update your app with new features, bug fixes, and improvements to provide the best possible user experience.

Conclusion

1- Here are some strategies to expedite your Flutter learning process:

1. Focus on fundamentals
2. Hands-on practice
3. Follow tutorials and guides
4. Join study groups
5. Set achievable goals

Q/A

2- How can I start making money with Flutter within a week of learning?

While earning money with Flutter within a week may be ambitious, here are some potential avenues to explore:

1. Freelance projects
2. Create Flutter templates
3. Build simple apps
4. Offer consulting services
5. Participate in hackathons

Q/A

3- What are some tips for maximizing my learning efficiency while studying Flutter?

Here are some tips to maximize your learning efficiency:

1. Create a structured learning plan
2. Use spaced repetition
3. Stay focused
4. Take breaks
5. Seek feedbac

Q/A

4- How can I overcome common challenges and roadblocks while learning Flutter?

Here are some strategies to overcome common challenges:

1. Persistence
2. Seek help
3. Break it down
4. Practice problem-solving
5. Embrace mistakes

Q/A

5- What are some strategies for balancing learning Flutter and making money simultaneously?

Balancing learning Flutter and making money requires effective time management and prioritization. Here are some strategies to achieve balance:

1. Set clear priorities
2. Establish a schedule
3. Optimize productivity
4. Leverage automation and tools
5. Stay flexible

140